INFOGRAPHICS

# THE ENCYCLOPEDIA OF GREAT INVENTIONS

## AMAZING INVENTIONS IN FACTS & FIGURES

BY TETIANA MASLOVA

ILLUSTRATED BY NATALIA BOLDYRIEVA

PUBLISHING HOUSE

RANOK

## The Encyclopedia of Great Inventions

**Amazing Inventions in Facts & Figures**

Series: Infographics for Kids

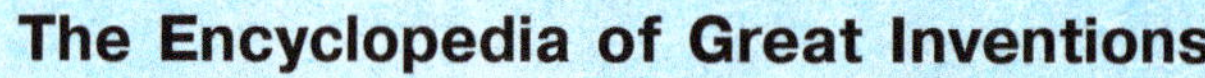






Created in 2018 by Encyclopedias team.
First published in 2018 by Publishing House Ranok Limited.
Redesigned for global publishing by Luda Werdin in 2019.
Luda Werdin is the official representative of Publishing House Ranok Limited authorized to act on its behalf.

ISBN: 978-617-09-5788-7

Publishing House Ranok Limited
135-27 Kibalchicha street, Kharkiv, Ukraine, 61071
"Encyclopedias" is a division of Publishing House Ranok Limited
For more information, contact "Encyclopedias",
21a Kosmichna street, Entrance 1, Floor 6,
Kharkiv, Ukraine, 61145
Email: office@ranok.com.ua
Edited by Anastasiia Tolmachova
Book design by Natalia Boldyrieva

# CONTENTS

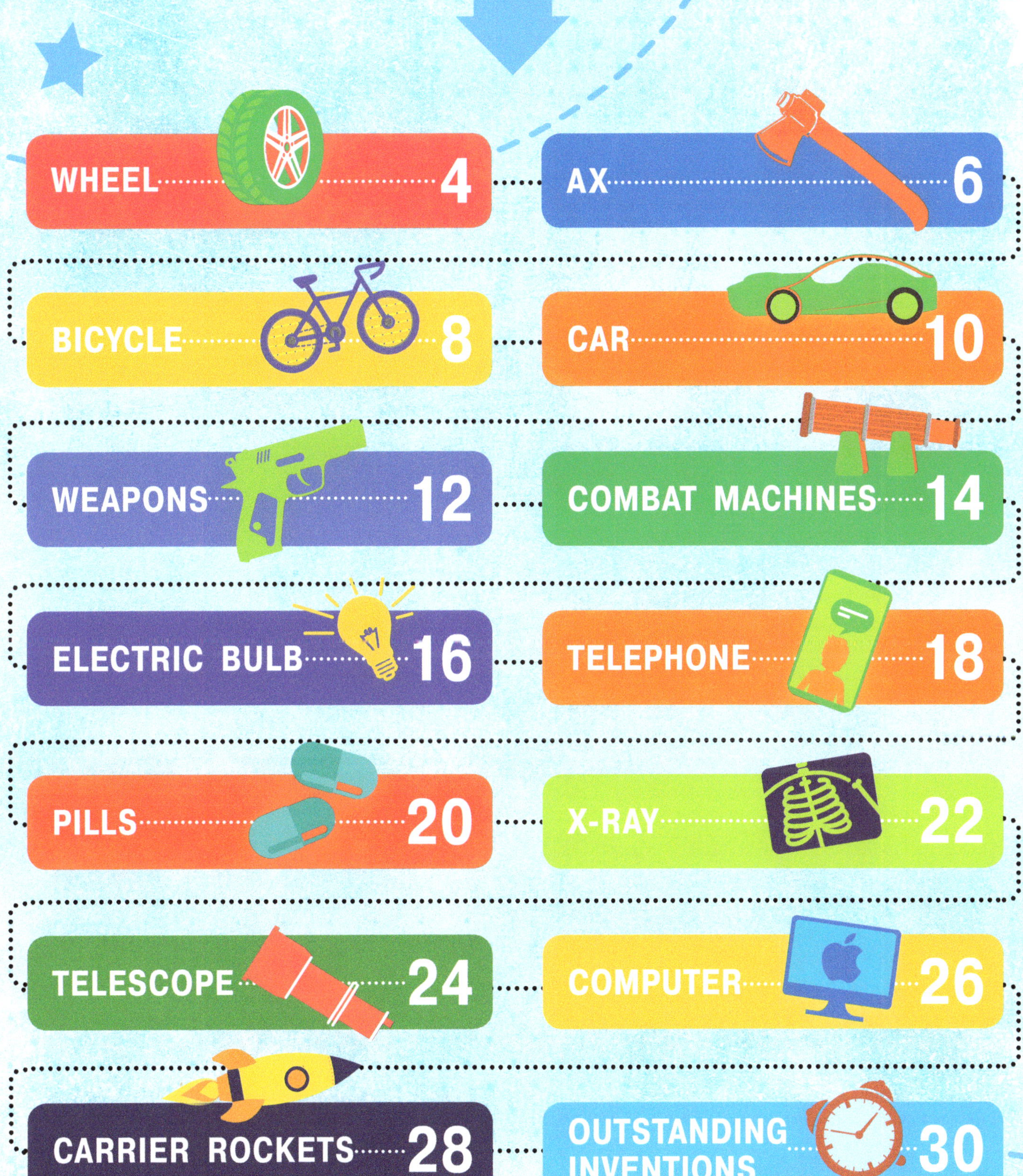

Heavy loads were very difficult to move by hand, so they were rolled with logs placed in rows. The wheel appeared when a narrow slice was cut out of the log. The wheel was gradually upgraded and made lighter by drilling holes in it. The hole in the center was used for inserting the axle, and the smaller holes around it made the wheel lighter.

## WHAT DOES THE CAR WHEEL CONSIST OF?

## COMPUTER MOUSE

In 1963, Douglas Engelbart invented the computer mouse. Initially, it had no scroll wheel. That was built in a bit later to make it easier to operate Windows.

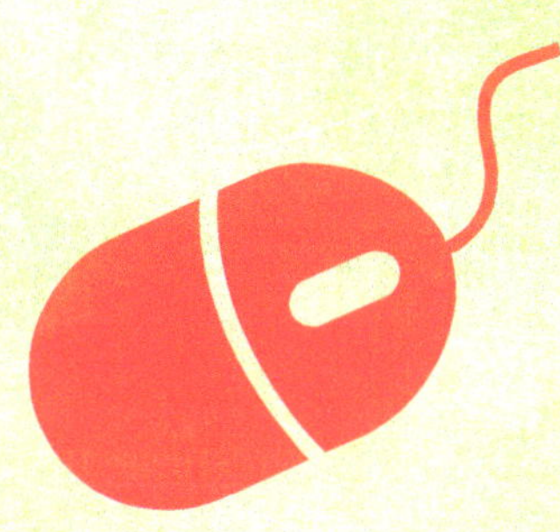

## MECHANICAL CLOCK

Mechanical clocks can work thanks to special cogwheels with cogs placed at their edges. With the help of those cogs, each cogwheel moves another one. Each of them has its own name: the central, the idler, the second, and the crutch cogwheels.

## "CURIOSITY" MARS ROVER

The "Curiosity" was launched by NASA in 2011. This "Martian explorer" continues work on the surface of Mars today. It moves with the help of 6 wheels, about 20 in. in diameter. The rover tires are made of aluminum, and the maximum speed it can gain is about 13 ft per second.

# AX

Ancient people had to get their food, build shelters, and hunt animals. It was about 1.5 million years ago that people invented the ax to accomplish those tasks. But it didn't look like our modern-day ax; it was an ordinary stone with one sharp edge — the so-called "cutter". Yet, fairly soon, people discovered how to attach the cutter to a wooden stick — the handle. Thus, the first stone ax appeared.

## THE BUILD OF THE AX



STONE-AGE HAND AX

AUSTRALIAN STONE AX

LABRYS – ANCIENT GREEK DOUBLE-BITTED AX

## "VTAC" TOMAHAWK

This light and handy ax was introduced to the US Stryker Brigade in 2003. With its help, soldiers can cut barbed wire, tear metal tanks open, and use it for self-defense in close-contact combat.

## FURNITURE

Modern axes not only help make furniture but also may become part of it. Thus, a London designer Chris Duffy, inspired with stories about Norwegian woodcutters, created an unusual table with legs of real axes. You needn't worry — the author guarantees you won't get cut with their blades.

## ICE AX

It's a special ax used by mountaineers while going up icy or snowy slopes. To be used conveniently and safely, it has a special strap called a sword-knot, which is attached to the climber's arm or harness.

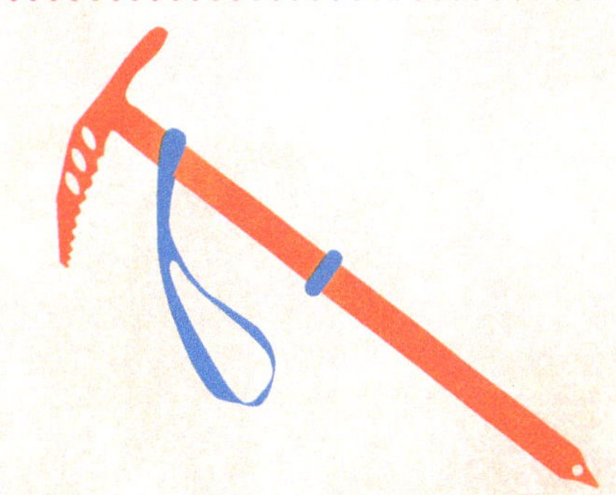

# BICYCLE

The bike's great-grandfather or the "running machine" appeared in 1817. It was invented by a German Karl Drais. The construction was very much like that of a scooter with handlebars and two wheels, which were connected with the help of a stick. The bicycle started looking like the one we know in 1885. Invented by the Englishman John Kemp Starley, it was called the "safety bicycle". The construction of the bike allowed the rider to keep balance while riding over potholes and bumps in the road. In addition, the bike had a chain-drive gear, which helped the wheels rotate.

## THE CONSTRUCTION OF A BICYCLE

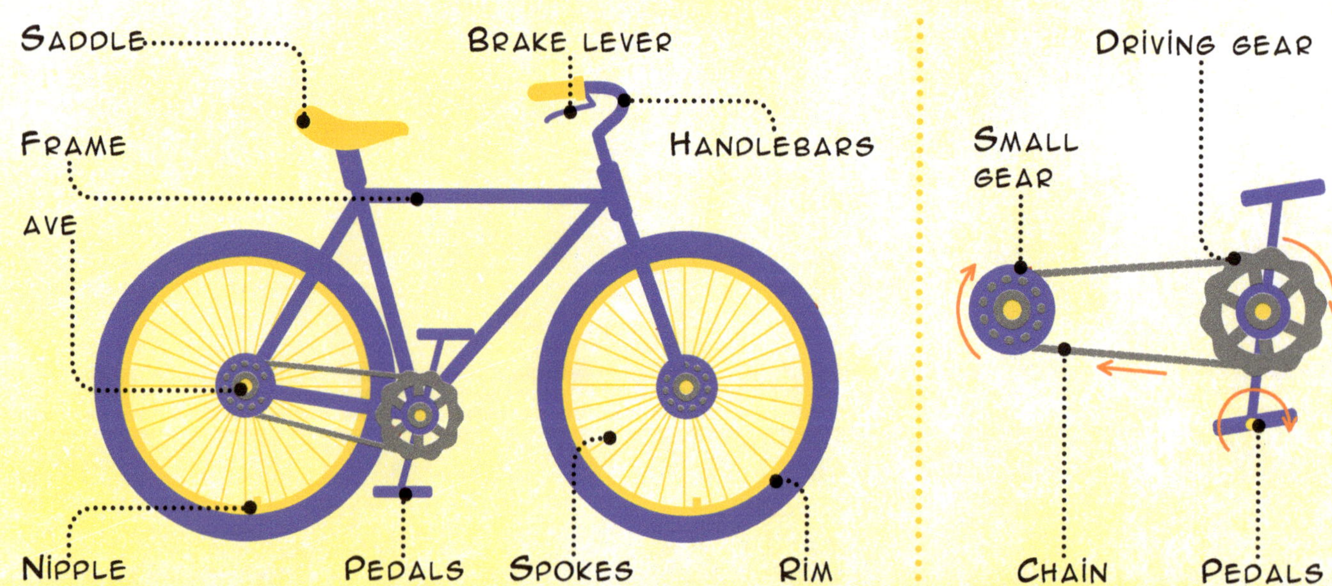

A bicycle can be used to literally ride around the world. The first journey of this kind was made by Fred Birchmore in 1935. He rode his bicycle across all of Asia, Europe, and the USA.

## TRICYCLE

A bike with three wheels is called a tricycle. Most often, such bikes are made for use by small children as this type of construction helps to keep better balance.

## HOVERBOARD

This transport resembles a scooter but it has no handlebars and works with the help of an electric motor. To ride a hoverboard, you don't have to push off from the ground — it's enough to just press your toes against the board — and it starts moving.

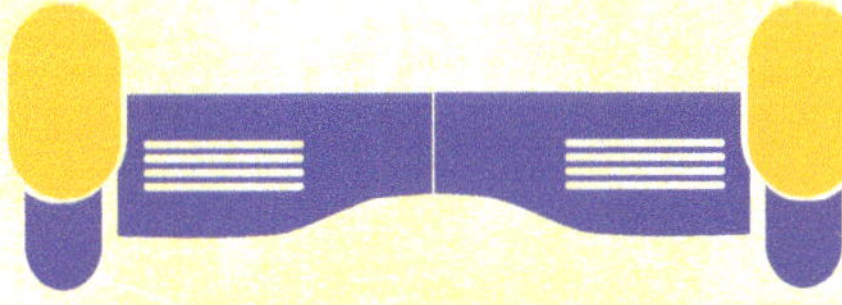



## SOLAR BATTERY BICYCLE

A bicycle that can work on solar energy was invented in Copenhagen, the capital of Denmark. The batteries are built in the bicycle wheels. By absorbing solar light, they charge the storage battery which will last up to 50 miles. But if the weather is cloudy, you'll have to pedal just like on a regular bicycle.

# CAR

Nowadays, the car has become a part of our everyday life. But once it really used to be the technology "wonder". Let's go back to 1886 when Gottlieb Daimler invented the first passenger car in the world by attaching an engine to a four-wheel carriage. That car had a steering wheel and a gas engine, and it was able to run as fast as about 11 mph. Later, in 1887, Gottlieb Daimler built the factory, which now is called "Mercedes-Benz".

## THE CONSTRUCTION OF A MODERN CAR

The first bus appeared in England in 1801, and it was created by Richard Trevithick. This kind of transport could hardly be called "public" as it could take only 8 passengers at once. What's more, it densely colored the city streets with steam engine fumes.

## "LIBERTY" – A FLYING CAR

The Aeromobile is a very convenient and simple vehicle, which lets you fly up high in the sky and then go along city streets. Upon landing, the roof propeller easily gets folded away, and we get a tricycle, which can run up to 100 mph.

## "TESLA MODEL 3"

This electric car works with the help of an electric motor and a storage battery and can run up to 300 miles if fully charged. "Tesla" company and its inspirer — the inventor Elon Musk are planning to have the entire world driving electric cars.

## "OPEL GT CONCEPT"

In 2016, "Opel" company presented the concept of the car of the future at the Geneva exhibition. The red lines on its body are the sensors, which help open the car doors. What's more, the car doesn't have side-view mirrors — they were replaced with cameras and monitors. The 'Opel GT Concept' can speed up to 135 mph.

# WEAPONS

## WHO INVENTED GUNPOWDER?

Nobody knows for sure who and when invented gunpowder. Scientists assume gunpowder first appeared in China around 5–6 centuries A.D. Then, some local "genius" mixed sulfur, charcoal, and saltpeter. This mixture not only burned well, but also exploded perfectly. But first, it was used in... fireworks. Yet, the military had their own plans for such "wonderful mix". They started using gunpowder in fireballs called "xo-pao" or "fire prickles". Europe was first introduced to gunpowder in the 13th century, and the first fire guns appeared in the 14th century. The Czech called them "piŝtals", from which later the word "pistol" appeared.

## THE KINDS OF FIREARMS

CHINESE FIREBALL

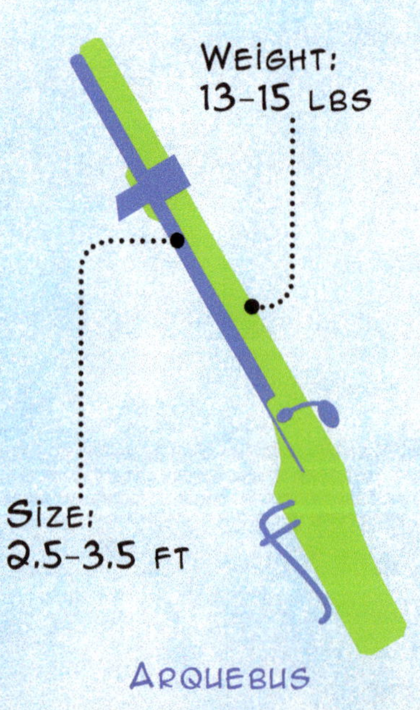


ARQUEBUS

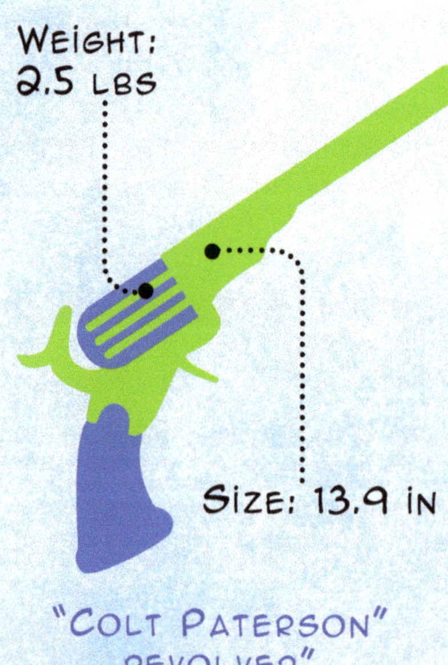


"COLT PATERSON" REVOLVER"

AMAZING FACTS


## ELON MUSK'S FLAMETHROWER

In 2017, the entrepreneur and inventor Elon Musk promised to start producing flamethrowers if he managed to sell 50 thousand baseball caps with his company logo.The caps were all bought and on January 28, 2018, the advance flamethrower ordering started. Musk wrote on his Twitter @elonmusk: "When the zombie apocalypse happens, you'll be glad you bought a flamethrower. Works against hordes of the undead or your money back!"

## "CORNER SHOT CSM"

The device enables a shooter to watch and shoot around the corner without leaving the shelter. The gun has the ability to become angle-shaped and it has both a handle and a surveillance monitor in the rear part. The front part contains a gun itself as well as fasteners for tactic lights.

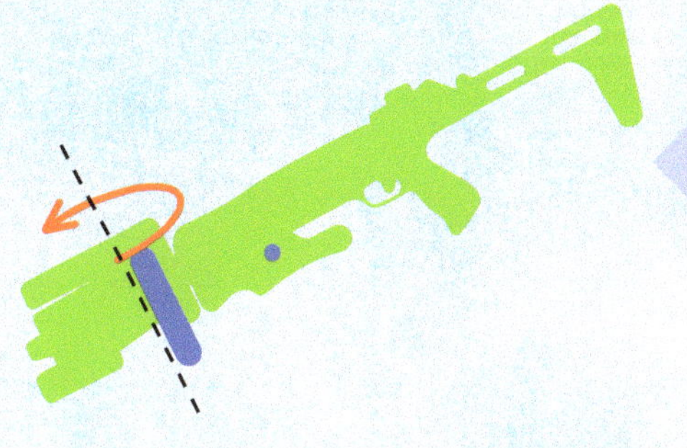


MODERN USE


## "TRACKINGPOINT" GUN

This gun was created in Texas. Now it is used by snipers for shooting long distances. There is a camera installed in the "TrackingPoint" which can record videos that can later be copied onto a smartphone or any other similar device.

# COMBAT MACHINES

It is believed that Greeks invented the first primitive flamethrower as long ago as in the 7th century. They made shells they called the "Greek fire". The first cannons appeared in Germany in the 16th century. They were named 'bombards', which came from Latin words: "bomb" – roar and "adere" – burn. Bombards were most often used when defending fortresses. But a serious breakthrough in the military sphere occurred during World War I when the English invented the tank.

## THE CONSTRUCTION OF COMBAT MACHINES

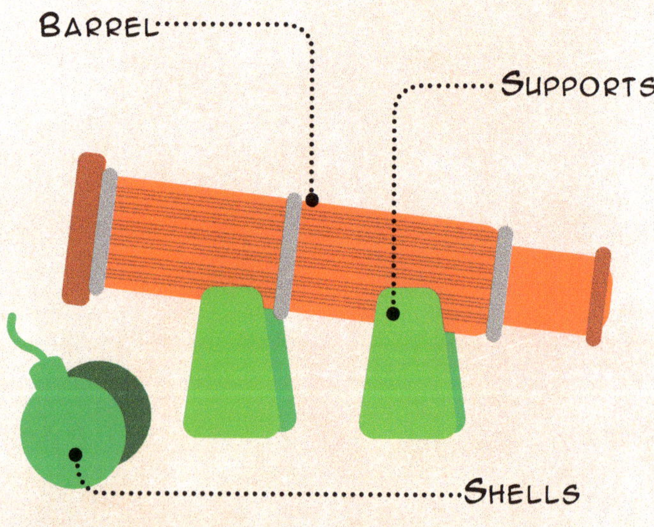


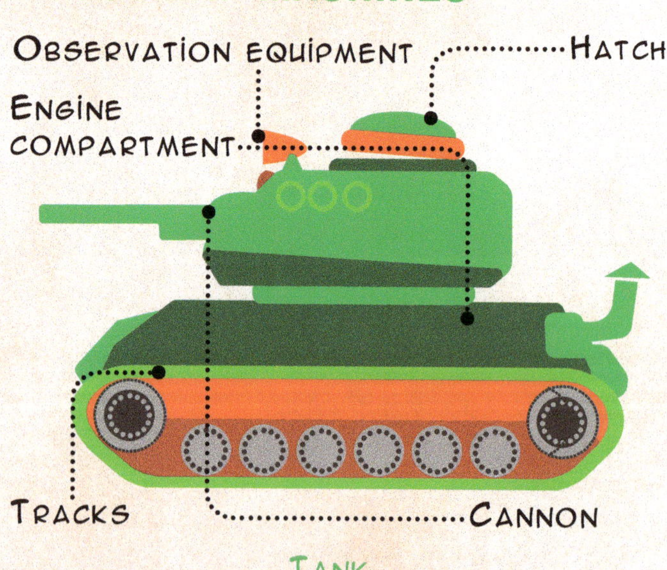

It's a common belief that tanks are huge and awkward machines. However, in the Guinness Book of Records, you can find a tank, which is barely 3 feet wide. It is a single-seated American tank named "Badger".

## "INVISIBLE TANK" PROJECT

In 2013, at the International Exhibition in Kielce, the Polish company "OBRUM" presented the concept of a future tank with a turret that could be controlled remotely. The tank got the name "invisible" because it's equipped with a system of heat camouflage. Such camouflage made it more difficult to detect by noctovisors.



## SOUTH KOREAN "K2 BLACK PANTHER"

The Republic of Korea is armed with the most expensive tank in the world – the "Black Panther". Its cost of $ 8,500,000 put it in the Guinness Book of Records. The built-in computer increases the accuracy of gunfire, and the maximum distance the tank can run fully fueled is about 280 miles.

# ELECTRIC BULB

Just imagine what life was like before the invention of the electric lamp: people had to light candles, kerosene lamps or gas lights. And that was very dangerous as it could cause fires! The inventors of the electric lamp we know today were the Russian Alexander Lodygin and the American Thomas Edison. In 1874, Lodygin invented a glow lamp with a coal filament. The filament, when heated to high temperatures, started emitting bright light. In the late 1870s, after a great number of experiments, Edison invented the lamp, which could work as long as 40 hours running! He also invented the socket, the plug, and even the lamp base and holder.

## THE CONSTRUCTION OF THE ELECTRIC BULB

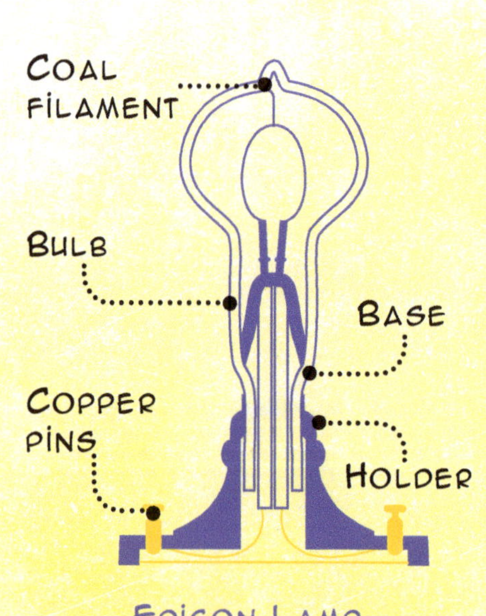


EDISON LAMP

INCANDESCENT LAMP

ENERGY-SAVING LAMP

It is believed that electric light bulbs deteriorate fairly quickly. However, in the state of California, there is an incandescent light bulb, which has been working for as long as 118 years! It has been put into the Guinness Book of Records as the world's longest-lasting light bulb.

## INCANDESCENT MIRROR LAMP

You may see such lamps in a shop window: their light is very bright and focused. The bulb in such lamps is partly covered with some mirror covering which reflects the light and doesn't let it disperse.

## STREET LAMPS

These lamps are used for lighting streets. They often have built-in motion sensors which turn the light on when somebody is approaching.

## PROJECTOR LAMP

The projectors in movie theaters also have lamps inside. They must be very bright to light such a large screen. For such purposes, xenon lamps are used — the light in them is emitted by the electric arc, and the bulb is filled with a special gas — xenon.

# TELEPHONE

Let's go back to the 19th century. It was then that the first ancestor of the telephone — the telegraph — appeared. It was invented by Samuel Morse. He also invented a special code, which enabled transmitting messages with the help of dot-and-dash signals. Later, Scottish Alexander Bell invented the device, which was named "telephone", and means "sound in the distance". The first telephones looked much different from the gadgets we know today. The telephone's "ancestors" were really huge and had lots of wires.

## THE CONSTRUCTION OF THE TELEPHONE

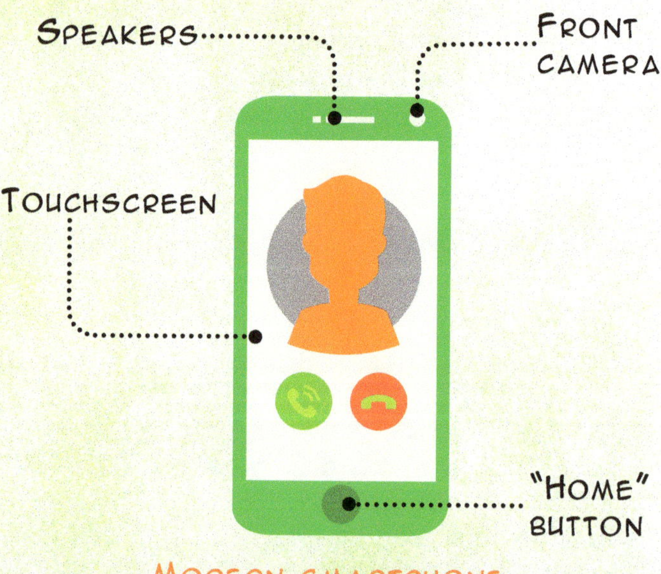

## IPHONE X

In 2017, "Apple" company presented the phone equipped with the "Face ID" technology. This technology "recognizes" the smartphone owner's face and unlocks the phone only if it 'recognizes' the face as the owner's. Such a function enables doing the shopping and being authorized for using internet applications.

## MODERN TECHNOLOGIES

Gadget programmers are constantly inventing something unusual. Thus, the leading manufacturers are planning to carry out such projects as flexible displays from LG, a 3D screen from Amazon, protecting the phone through scanning the retina from Samsung. These projects are currently being improved so that consumers can enjoy the new functions in the nearest future.

# PILLS

## HOW COULD PEOPLE DO WITHOUT PILLS?

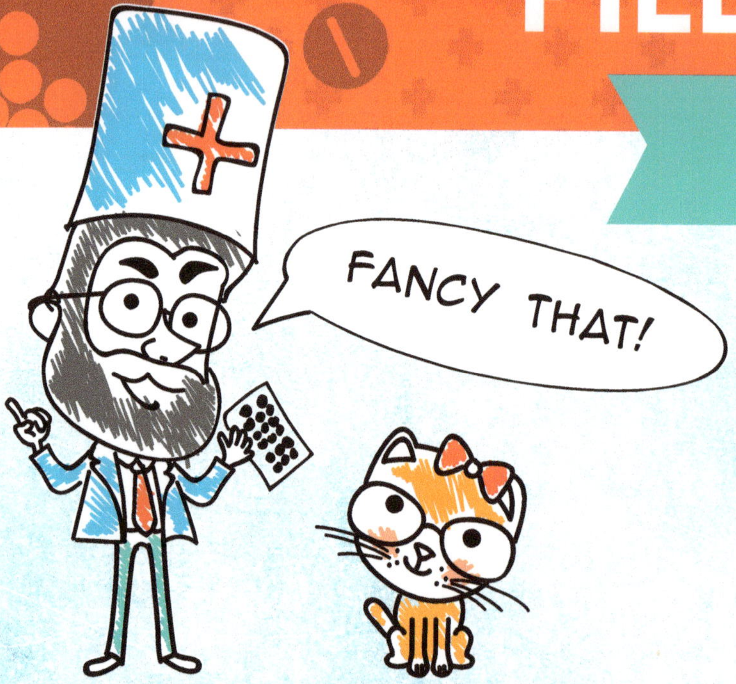

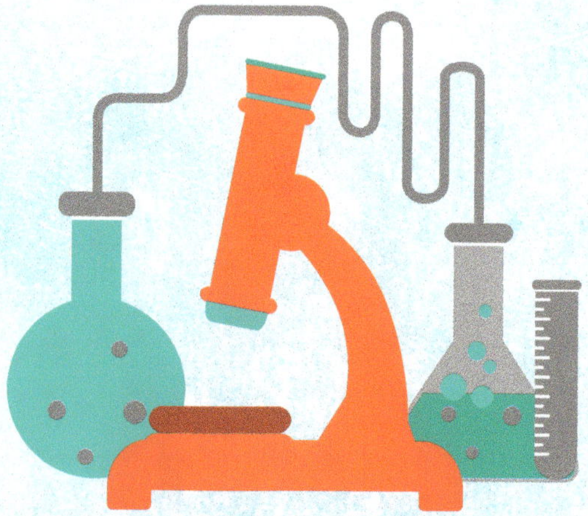

In every home, we can find a medicine cabinet with many pills, ointments, and syrups. They all help us when we are sick. But how did our ancestors do without such assistants? In ancient times, people knew a lot more about the medicinal characteristics of plants. Ancient doctors pounded special medicinal plants, made herbal potions or boiled them in vinegar to extract all the useful components. Doctors made mixtures and tinctures, which helped heal diseases, burns, and wounds. The first pills appeared in the 16th century when the Swiss doctor Paracelsus moistened and pressed medical powder. And in the mid-19th century, the first machines that produced the pills we know today appeared.

### HOW PILLS WORK

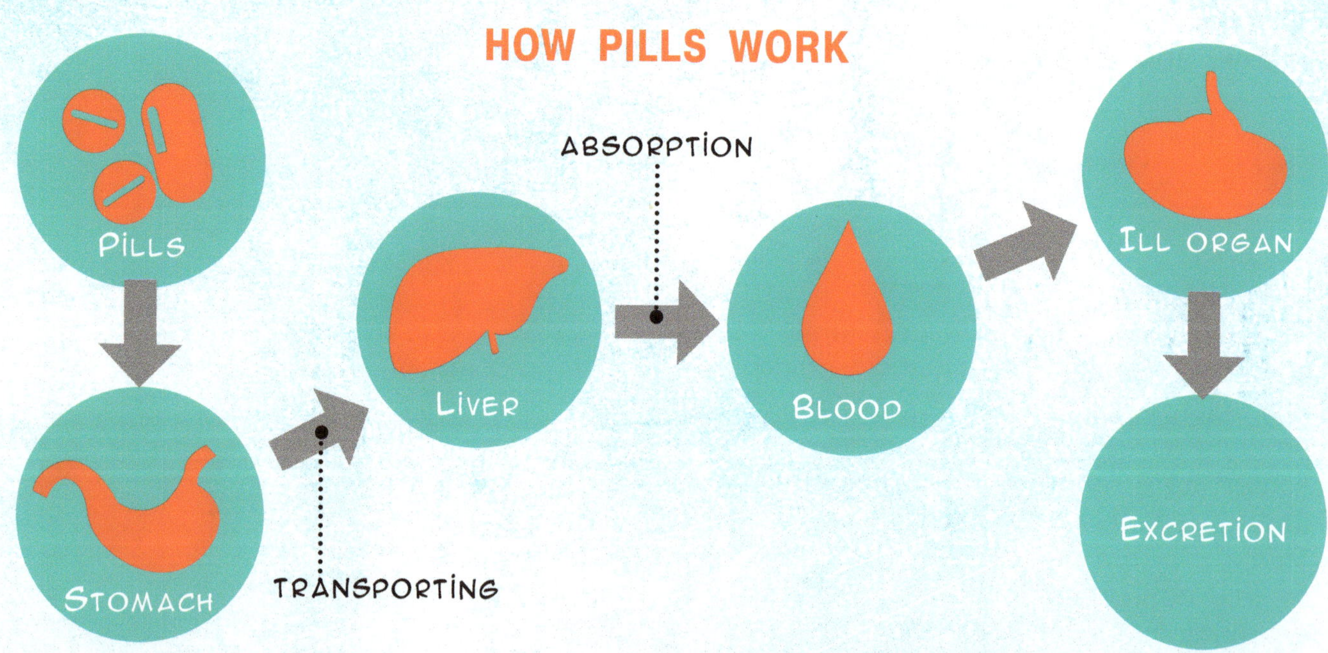

Even though pharmacology has already made great advances, plants are still used for treatment purposes. And it's no wonder, as our planet houses more than 12 thousand plants, which may be helpful for treating various diseases.



## CHEWABLE PILLS

Such medicine will be to the liking of those who don't like swallowing pills because you can just chew them. They are usually quite tasty, smell good and remind us of candy. Yet, you should remember that any pills, even the tastiest ones, must be taken only with a doctor's prescription.

## CAPSULE MEDICINES

Medicines in special soluble capsules help the body to assimilate them: the capsule is dissolved in the stomach, and then the medicine moves further and is absorbed by another organ — the pancreas.

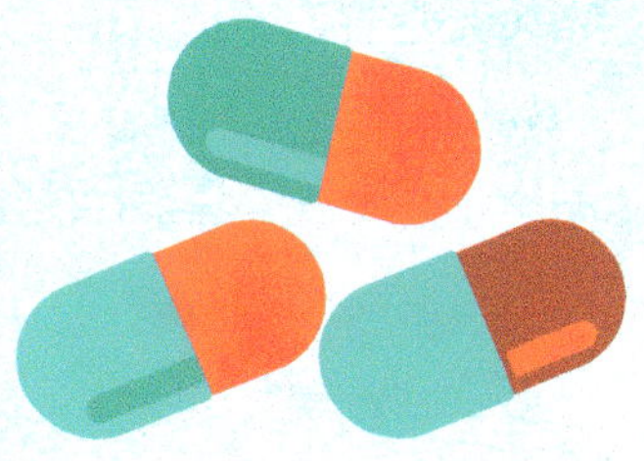



## SYRUPS

Most syrups have a pleasant smell and a sweetish taste. They start "working" in the body much faster than pills because the medicine is already dissolved.

## HOW DID X-RAYS APPEAR?

You might have heard the word "X-rays" before. And, most likely, you know that it helps to take "pictures" of a person's or animal's skeleton and internal organs. It appeared more than 100 years ago. In 1895, a German Wilhelm Roentgen was experimenting with an electronic tube. For one of the probes, he put black cardboard around the tube and darkened the room. Then he turned the tube on. A photo plate in his laboratory started glowing. He showed his discovery to his wife: he took her hand, placed it under the rays, and took a picture. His wife was quite surprised as she could see the bones of her hand! Wilhelm Roentgen gave the rays the name "X-rays'.

## THE CONSTRUCTION OF AN X-RAY MACHINE

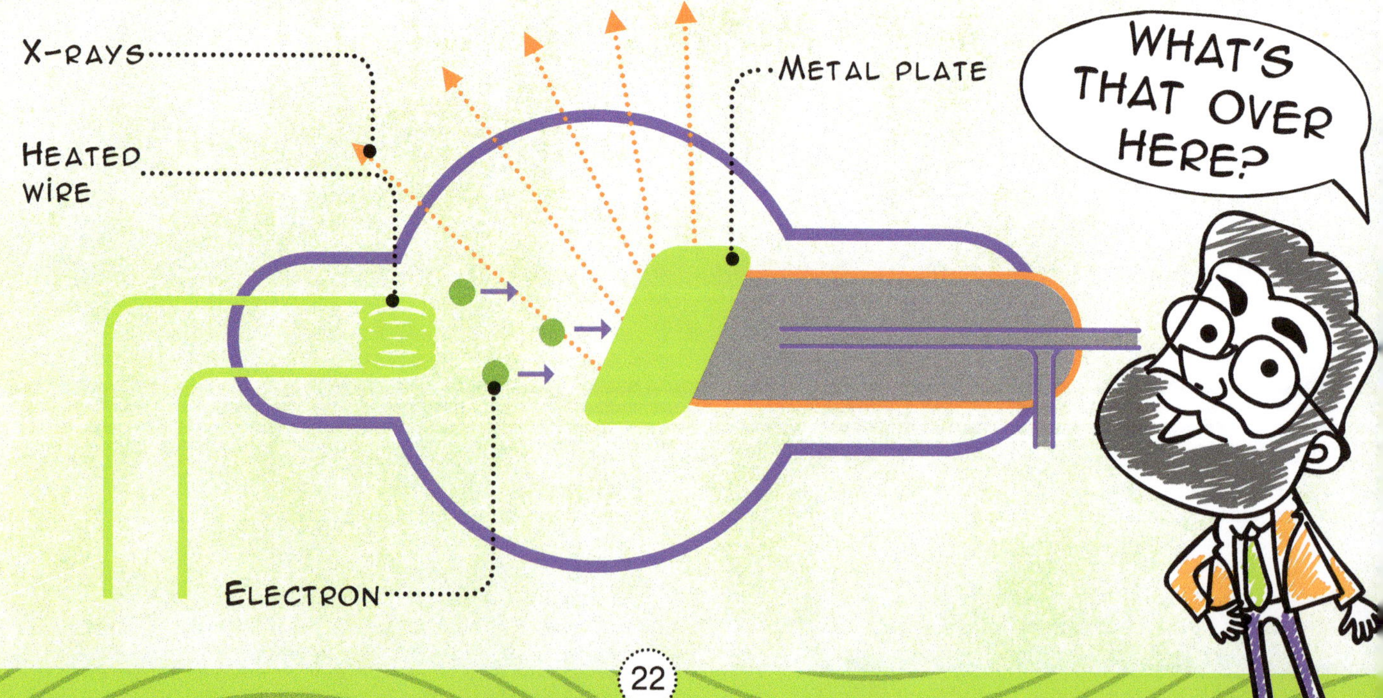

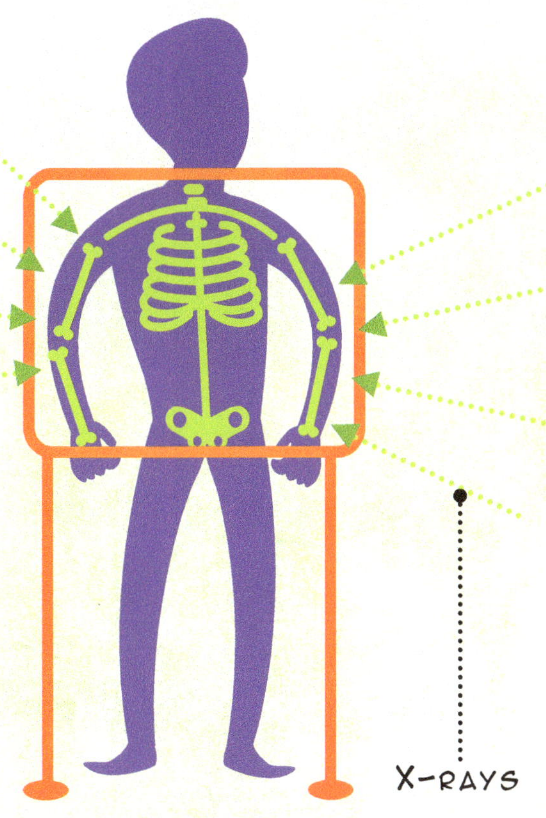


When people started using X-rays in medicine, it turned out the X-rays could produce the same skin burns as the sunlight does. But this problem was resolved very quickly — by reducing the dose and the time of exposure to those rays.



## AT THE AIRPORT

X-rays are used for scanning the baggage and packages at airports. This guarantees safety: the airport staff knows for sure there are no forbidden items on board the plane.

## ORIGINAL PAINTING?

To find the original of the picture, X-rays are used. First, the pictures of both paintings are taken, and then experts determine how the paints were applied.

## X-RAY ASTRONOMY

With the help of special telescopes built with the use of X-ray technology, scientists can observe stars because celestial bodies emit X-rays.

# TELESCOPE

People have always dreamed of flying above the skies, to find out what there is beyond the Sun, and even to touch a star... Today, with the help of the most powerful telescopes, we are able to see what is beyond the Solar system and to observe the surfaces of other planets. But the first telescope in the world wasn't capable of doing that: it could only provide triple magnification. The telescope was invented by the Italian Galileo Galilei in 1609. He aimed the telescope in the sky and saw the Moon closer than anyone else.

## THE CONSTRUCTION OF THE TELESCOPE

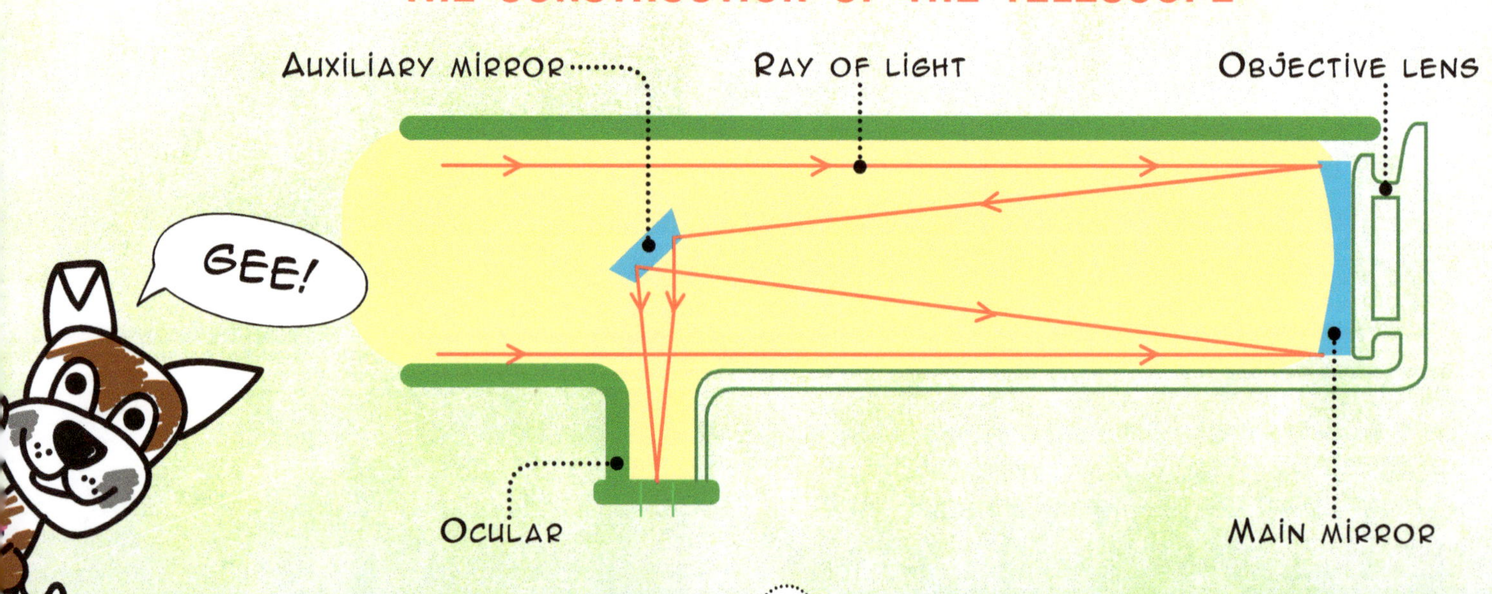

## OBSERVATORY

An observatory is an exciting place where we can literally "make acquaintance" with stars with the help of powerful telescopes. One of the most beautiful and most visited observatories in the world is in France and has the name "Pic du Midi Observatory". Both tourists and scientists are attracted by its incredible 27-feet dome, the cableway leading to the facilities, and the powerful 42-inch telescope.



## GIANT MAGELLAN TELESCOPE

Since 2012, a giant telescope has been under construction in Chile: it is supposed to have 7 huge mirrors each weighing 20 tons. The construction should be finished in 2020 after which the telescope will be located in a sparsely populated area of Chile because that area has the least polluted environment and the cleanest air throughout the year.

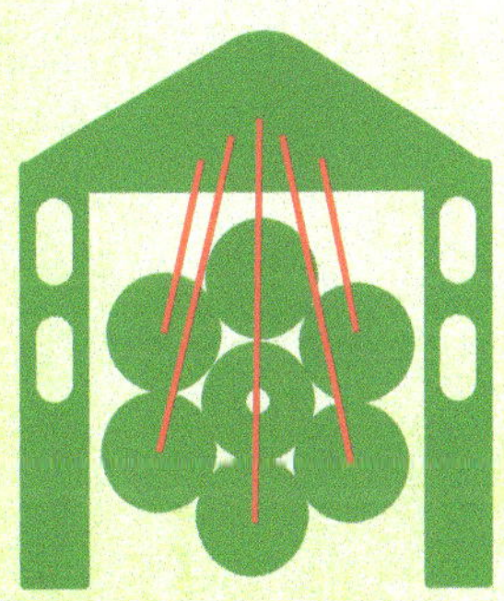

## 100-FT TELESCOPE

A telescope with a giant mirror of 100 feet in diameter is going to be built on the Canary Islands pretty soon! This telescope is supposed to study the nature of black matter, black holes, the formation of galaxies, and will answer other questions concerning the Universe.

## GREAT RESEARCH TELESCOPE

The world's largest research telescope is projected for completion by 2024. It's being built on Mt Sierra-Pachón in Chile. The telescope will take panoramic photos of the night sky and make a map of the Milky Way.

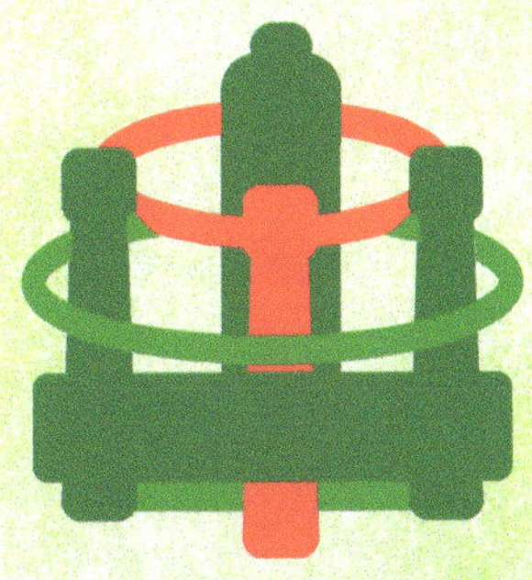

# COMPUTER

## HOW DID THE COMPUTER APPEAR?

The history of the computer is full of discoveries, inventions, unbelievable falls and unexpected rises. Let's move back to 1945. It was in the middle of the 20th century that the first electronic calculating machine – ENIAC was created. I bet if you saw it today you'd never guess it was a computer. The first electronic calculating machine was huge: it occupied a whole room and weighed 27 tons! It was created by Americans Presper Eckert and John Mauchly who made it for calculating ballistic tables. Data input was performed by means of special punch cards and punch tapes.

## THE CONSTRUCTION OF THE COMPUTER

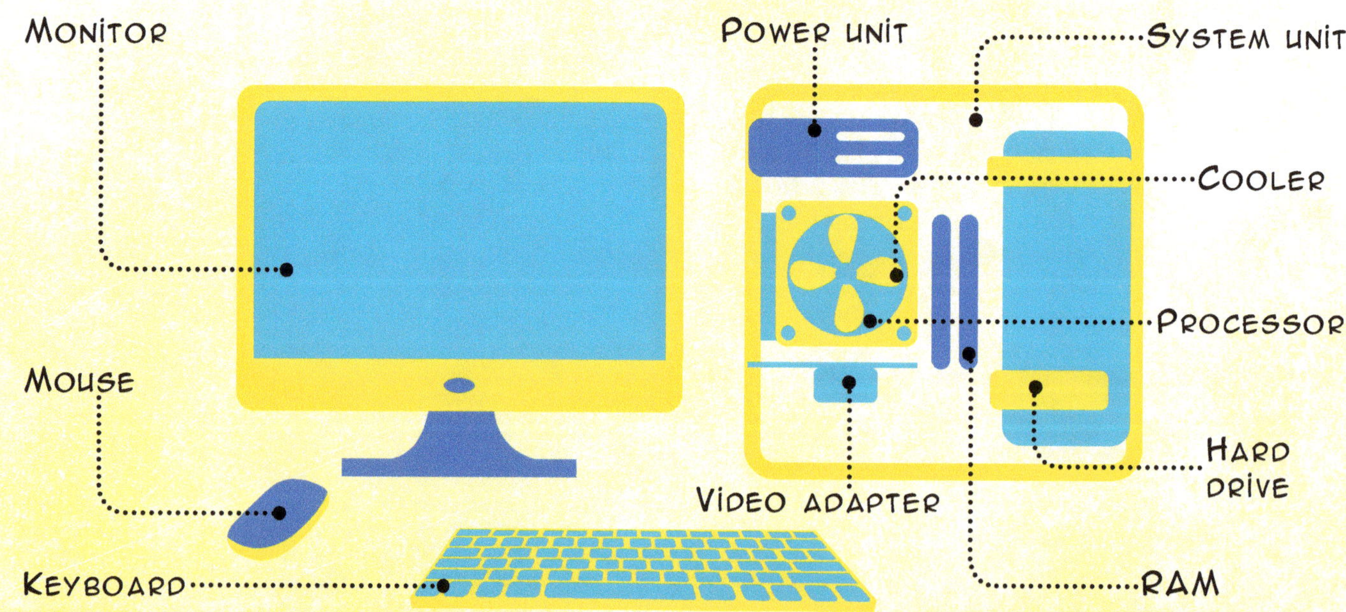

Standard Windows games such as "Solitaire", "Minesweeper", and "Chess" didn't appear in the system just for entertainment. The developers made them part of the system when a computer mouse was invented. Thus, the designers wanted to help users figure out how the mouse worked and how it could be operated.

## "Q-STICK" MINICOMPUTER

This minicomputer can be easily placed onto the palm of your hand or put into your pocket. It enables you to listen to music, work with a variety of applications or browse the internet. To be able to work with it, the Q-Stick should be connected to a monitor or TV.

## THE MOST POWERFUL COMPUTER IN THE WORLD

The most powerful computer in the world as of today was developed by American scientists from IBM for use at Oak Ridge National Laboratory. Its official name is "Summit". The computer's capability is 200 petaflops (operations per second), which is more than twice as much as the capability of the latest Chinese Sunway TaihuLight supercomputer.

## "IMAC PRO"

The modern computer by "Apple" is not a supercomputer yet, but as of today, it is one of the most powerful ones. A 27-inch display supports more than a billion colors. What's more, it has an 18-nucleus processor and the RAM of 64 Gb.

# CARRIER ROCKETS

An attempt to build the first carrier rocket took place in 1939. British scientists wanted to make a rocket to send cargo to the Moon. But lack of necessary technology did not make it possible then. To put a space flight to life was a success of Soviet scientists: in 1957 they managed to launch a "P-7" rocket with cargo in it onto the orbit of the Earth. And the first manned space flight took place on April 12, 1961 on the spaceship "Vostok-1" with Yuri Gagarin on board. The flight orbited the Earth in 108 minutes.

## THE CONSTRUCTION OF THE ROCKET

## FALCON HEAVY

The American super-heavy rocket, which was designed by the SpaceX company headed by Elon Musk, was launched into space on February, 6, 2018. The rocket set the "Tesla Roadster" electric car with a dummy as a driver into orbit. Alongside with the car, a drive with Isaac Asimov's "Foundation" series was sent into space. The drive can stand up to +1830 ℉, and at + 375℉, it can remain intact for 13.8 billion years.

## DELTA-4

This is an American carrier rocket used for launching satellites into the Earth's orbit. It is used by the US Department of Defense and US intelligence. The carrier rocket was first launched in 2002, and in 2004 it brought the "Orion" spaceship into orbit. NASA is planning to use it for further missions to the Moon and Mars.

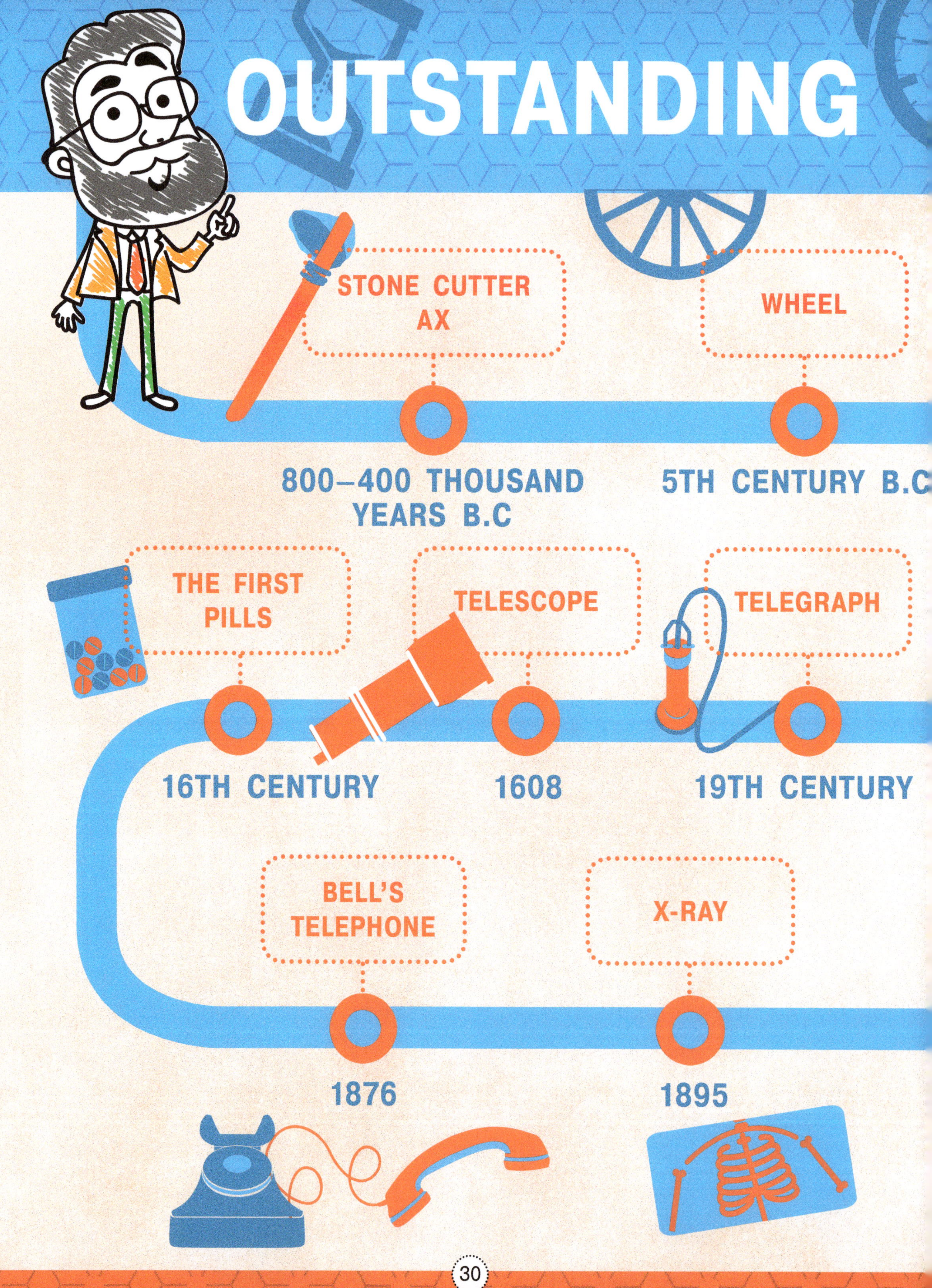

OUTSTANDING
STONE CUTTER AX
WHEEL
800–400 THOUSAND YEARS B.C
5TH CENTURY B.C
THE FIRST PILLS
TELESCOPE
TELEGRAPH
16TH CENTURY
1608
19TH CENTURY
BELL'S TELEPHONE
X-RAY
1876
1895

# INVENTIONS

**GUNPOWDER**

**GREEK FLAMETHROWER**

**BOMBARD**

**5TH–6TH CENTURY A.D**

**7TH CENTURY A.D.**

**16TH CENTURY**

**THE FIRST BICYCLE**

**ELECTRIC LAMP**

**1817**

**1874**

**THE FIRST CARRIER ROCKET**

**ENIAC ELECTRONIC CALCULATING MACHINE**

**1939**

**1945**